PEARL GIDLEY

PEARL GIDLEY

GARY KIRKHAM

Pearl Gidley
first published 2012 by
Scirocco Drama
An imprint of J. Gordon Shillingford Publishing Inc.

Scirocco Drama Editor: Glenda MacFarlane
Cover design by Terry Gallagher/Doowah Design Inc.
Author photo by Tory Vimmerman
Printed and bound in Canada on 100% post-consumer recycled paper.

We acknowledge the financial support of the Manitoba Arts Council and The Canada Council for the Arts for our publishing program.

Production inquiries should be addressed to:
Charles Northcote, Core Literary Inc.
140 Wolfrey Avenue
Toronto, ON M4K 1L3
416-466-4929
charlesnorthcote@rogers.com

Library and Archives Canada Cataloguing in Publication

Kirkham, Gary., 1962-
Pearl Gidley / Gary Kirkham.

A play.
ISBN 978-1-897289-79-2

I. Title.

PS8621.I738P42 2012 C812'.6 C2012-904729-5

J. Gordon Shillingford Publishing
P.O. Box 86, RPO Corydon Avenue, Winnipeg, MB Canada R3M 3S3

Acknowledgments

Special thanks to the keepers of the Blyth archives, Brock and Janice Vodden, who introduced me to the real story of Pearl Gidley over instant coffee.

Thank you to Tony McQuail who invited me into his home and told me a heart-wrenching story that inspired the soul of the play.

Special thanks to the Blyth Festival and Eric Coates for making it happen. To my dream cast Katerine, Pat, Gil and Sam. And to the wonderful Miles Potter who pushed me ever so hard to write a better script.

There are numerous artists that helped bring the play alive. Thanks to Kathleen Sheehy, Alan K. Sapp, Jen Cornish, Brad Cook, Gord Cameron, Marion Day, Peggy Coffey, Terry Barna, and of course Chea Kirkham.

The play was developed thanks to a grant by the Ontario Arts Council's Playwright Residency program.

Characters

Pearl Gidley, late 60s

Edith Gidley, late 60s

George, 40-50s

Andrew, 22

The Set

Pearl's and Edith's home. It is a large house that has seen better days. There is a living room and dining room area with the entrance to the kitchen on one side, a hallway leading to the front door on the other. There is a set of stairs going up. The exterior is a small side porch with a door to the house. There is a well-made piano that overwhelms the room. Most of the furniture is from the '20s. There is a small sitting area and dining room table that seats 6 (or 4).

Location and Time

Small Ontario town. Autumn 1969.

Production History

Pearl Gidley was first produced by the Blyth Fesitval on July 30, 2010, with the following cast and crew:

PEARL..Catherine Fitch

EDITH..Patricia Hamilton

ANDREW...Gil Garratt

GEORGE..Sam Malkin

Directed by Miles Potter

Set and Costume Design by Gillian Gallow

Lighting Design by Steve Lucas

Sound Design by Todd Charlton

Stage Manager: Shauna Japp

Assistant Stage Manager: Crystal MacDonell

Artistic Director: Eric Coates

Gary Kirkham

Gary Kirkham is an actor and playwright based in Cambridge, Ontario. In addition to *Pearl Gidley* his writing credits include *Queen Milli of Galt* (Winner of the S.F. Canadian Playwriting Award), *Pocket Rocket* (with Lea Daniel), and *Falling: A Wake* which was recently translated into Italian. Gary is a member of the MT Space and has worked in collaboration with the company on several show including *Seasons of Immigration, Body 13, Occupy Spring,* and the critically acclaimed *The Last 15 Seconds*. He authored an adaptation of Easter bu August Strindberg. His plays have had over 40 productions across Canada, the United States and the Middle East. He was Playwright-in-Residence at the Blyth Festival in 2008.

Act I

Tuning the Piano

Before the start of the play there is the sound of a very well made piano being tuned.

The notes being hit should be subtly musical but still the sound of a piano being tuned. (Think John Cage.)

Lights up:

It is the afternoon in late fall.

PEARL is wearing a plain, dull-colored dress and has her hair in a bun. She is listening to the tuning from the side porch.

Inside the home, we see a man, in shadow, tuning the piano.

The tuning stops.

There is a silence.

PEARL waits.

There is the tender sound of Brahms' transcription for piano for left hand only of Chaconne from J.S. Bach's "Partita."

She listens to it, it's full of longing…

The playing stops.

We see the player, his name is GEORGE. He is in his

50s, with cerebral palsy, [(Spastic hemiplegia) right side only affected]. He looks elegant and disheveled at the same time.

GEORGE picks up his wooden tool box and hobbles to the side porch. He looks at PEARL who stands motionless...frozen.

GEORGE: Done.

PEARL doesn't move.

Miss Gidley? *(Pause.)*

PEARL stares blankly at GEORGE.

I...I finished tuning. I softened the felt a bit. The keys were stiff so I loosened them up. She was mostly in tune, so I didn't have to do that much. She's ready to be played. *(Pause.)* Well. Goodbye Miss Gidley.

GEORGE starts to exit.

PEARL: I thought I told you not to play the piano!

GEORGE: I'm sorry?

PEARL: I told you not to play the piano!

GEORGE: Yes, Miss Gidley. It's hard to tune it if I can't play it.

PEARL: You could have played notes! You didn't have to play a tune!

GEORGE: I felt sorry for the (piano)...sorry. *(Pause.)* Goodbye Miss Gidley.

GEORGE starts to exit again.

PEARL: "Chaconne"? (*Sha-kon'*)

GEORGE: Hmmm?

PEARL: The tune, "Chaconne"?

GEORGE: You know it? There's not much music written for one hand. Brahms must've had a friend who was a gimp.

PEARL: I had no idea you could play so well.

GEORGE: I can't.

PEARL: (Sorry?)

GEORGE: I only play the one piece, and...and just the first minute. I never took lessons. I never found a teacher patient enough to teach me. I taught myself to play it by ear.

I play it once every day. Maybe in five more years it will sound good. *(Beat.)* Miss Gidley I'm sorry I—

PEARL: —Now, you have to promise to cash the cheque. *(Handing GEORGE an envelope.)*

GEORGE: Humph.

PEARL: George? When I called you, you said you would cash the cheque.

He puts the envelope in his pocket.

GEORGE: No, I said I would cash the cheque if you played the piano.

PEARL: It's been played.

GEORGE: Humph.

PEARL: What?

He takes out a two dollar bill from his pocket.

What is that?

GEORGE: Proof.

PEARL: Proof of what?

GEORGE: Proof you haven't played the piano. *(Pause.)* I put this two dollar bill between the middle C strings the last time I tuned it. That was a year ago.

PEARL: *(Snapping.)* If I choose not to play it, that's my business.

GEORGE: It's a beautiful piano, it needs to be played.

PEARL: Goodbye George.

GEORGE: One note.

PEARL: Pardon me?

GEORGE: Just play one note a day. Do you think you could do that? *(Pause.)* Do it for the piano.

PEARL: *(Pause.)* Goodbye George!

PEARL goes inside and slams the door.

GEORGE: One note.

GEORGE picks up his tool case and starts to leave.

He stops. He turns back and opens the screen door. It squeaks. He takes out a tin of 3-in-1 oil from his tool box and lubricates the hinge. He puts the oil in the tool box and starts to leave again.

EDITH (PEARL's sister) enters the side porch. She is in her late 60s, dressed immaculately in a classic '50s style. She is carrying a paper grocery bag.

EDITH: George?

GEORGE: Good afternoon.

EDITH: What are you doing here?

He holds up his tool box.

Oh dear. Pearl? Where's Pearl?

GEORGE: Inside.

EDITH: How was she?

GEORGE: She snapped at me.

EDITH: Good.

GEORGE: Not if you're the one being snapped at. It's my favourite—Pearl's piano—I really enjoy tuning it.

EDITH: What a waste of money.

GEORGE: Oh…

EDITH: No, I'm not saying… Sorry. It's just Pearl doesn't…

GEORGE: I know.

EDITH: Every year she has it tuned. And every year…

GEORGE: It looks like it hasn't been played in ten years .

EDITH: Longer…much longer.

GEORGE: And after playing Carnegie Hall.

EDITH: She never played Carnegie Hall.

GEORGE: I've been telling people for years that I know someone who played Carnegie Hall.

EDITH: So it was you that started that rumour!

GEORGE: No, I heard it when I first moved here. I just kept the rumour alive.

EDITH: Well, she did play Massey Hall, and Memorial Hall and then…

GEORGE: And then?

EDITH: She stopped.

GEORGE: Maybe you can convince her to sell it. It's worth several—

EDITH: No! *(Pause.)* Several…? Several hundred?

GEORGE: Thousand. Well… Three, maybe four thousand.

EDITH: That's more than a house.

GEORGE: I can put the word out, see if anyone wants to buy it.

EDITH: No. Thank you George.

GEORGE: Hmmm…

EDITH: What?

GEORGE: Nothing.

EDITH: You're thinking something.

GEORGE: I am?

EDITH: George?

GEORGE: You have a boarder?

EDITH: We haven't had a boarder for…hmmm… We don't have a boarder.

GEORGE: Things are tight all over.

EDITH: You're looking for a room?

GEORGE: Yes.

EDITH: Did Charlene kick you out again?

GEORGE: Um…

EDITH: Oh dear, I'm so sorry. I forgot she was… Sorry.

GEORGE: No, no I forget too. Yesterday I walked into the shop and said "I'm back" ...Hmmm... Sometimes it's nice to forget.

EDITH: She'll be missed... She was fortunate to have someone who misses her.

GEORGE looks at EDITH who is quite moved.

We're all dying George.

GEORGE: "He not busy being born, is busy dying."

EDITH: Yes, hmmm... Who said that ?

GEORGE: Dylan.

EDITH: Dylan?

GEORGE: The folk singer.

EDITH: The Jew.

GEORGE: Um... Yeah.

EDITH: Hmmm... You need a room?

GEORGE: Yes, I have a friend. He's looking for a place to stay for a few days.

EDITH: Hmm...it would be nice to—we could use the money. We could certainly use the money. What's his name?

GEORGE: Hmmm?

EDITH: Your friend. What's his name?

GEORGE: Umm.

EDITH: He's your friend and you don't know his name?

GEORGE: He's a friend of a friend.

EDITH: One of your communist friends?

GEORGE: The NDP is not communist.

EDITH: Where's he from?

GEORGE: United States.

EDITH: He's not one of those…those… (what do they call them?)

GEORGE: No, he's not a draft dodger.

EDITH: George… Maybe find someone else to take him in.

GEORGE: Just a few days.

EDITH: I don't want to be involved in one of your… whatever you are up to, I don't want to be involved. I don't want trouble.

GEORGE: No no…this is something good…very good.

EDITH: Why don't you take him in?

GEORGE: I live in my shop, I don't cook. He needs a home. A nice home.

EDITH: *(Pause.)* I don't know…

GEORGE: Thank you.

GEORGE hands EDITH the cheque.

EDITH: I said, I don't know.

GEORGE: I heard.

EDITH: *(Looking at cheque.)* That's a week's worth.

GEORGE: You're doing me a favour.

EDITH: I'm trusting you George.

GEORGE: I'm trustworthy.

EDITH: I know. *(Pause.)* Pearl doesn't need to know about— well, whatever it is that we are not talking about, she needn't know.

GEORGE: I'll bring him by tomorrow. *(Pause.)* Thank you for being…

EDITH: An accomplice?

GEORGE: For being good.

EDITH: Humph, we'll see.

GEORGE exits.

EDITH goes into the house.

She sees PEARL who seems lost.

Pearl dear? *(Pause.)* Pearl!

PEARL: Ahh, you're back.

EDITH: Yes. *(Pause.)* I spoke to George.

PEARL: Oh.

EDITH: I thought we talked about this.

PEARL: We talked, but we didn't decide.

EDITH: Such a waste!

PEARL: (What?)

EDITH: Tuning that piano. Such a waste of money.

PEARL: If it's not tuned every year it will become useless.

EDITH: It is useless. Sitting there. What good is it? *(Pause.)* I bought you some tea.

PEARL: Hmmm?

EDITH: Tea. I bought you some tea. Lapsang.

PEARL: Thank you Edee.

EDITH shows PEARL a tin of tea.

You found Lapsang Souchong?

EDITH: Yes.

PEARL: Stewart's is selling Lapsang tea?

EDITH: No. I got it at Benson's.

PEARL: You went to Benson's?

EDITH: Yes.

PEARL: You went all the way to Goderich.

EDITH: I was already in town.

PEARL: I thought you were going to the shut-in.

EDITH: Yes, I did.

PEARL: The shut-in is in Goderich?

EDITH: *(Pause.)* Yes.

PEARL: You've been driving all the way to—

EDITH: It's only half an hour's drive.

PEARL: Surely there is a church there that can take care of shut-ins.

EDITH: Yes, but he doesn't know anyone there…he's from— He's not from Goderich.

PEARL: I hope you're not the only one.

EDITH: Hmmm?

PEARL: Driving… I hope the others take turns driving.

EDITH: Yes… I'll make some tea.

PEARL: No, sit down, I'll make it.

EDITH: I don't mind.

PEARL: Well I do.

EDITH: What?

PEARL: I don't like the way you make tea.

EDITH: There is only one way to make tea.

PEARL: That's why I never let you make it.

PEARL exits.

EDITH looks at the piano.

Fade to black.

We Have a Visitor

It is the afternoon of the next day.

PEARL is standing at the dining room table looking at a bunch of papers strewn about.

PEARL: Have you found it? *(Pause.)* Edith?

EDITH: *(O.S.)* What's that?

PEARL: DID YOU FIND IT?

EDITH: *(O.S.)* Looking.

PEARL: If you can't find it. It doesn't matter.

EDITH: *(O.S.)* What did you say?

PEARL: DID YOU FIND IT?

EDITH: *(O.S.)* Coming.

EDITH enters from the kitchen with an old hat box.

PEARL: DO YOU WANT ME TO LOOK?

EDITH: You needn't yell.

PEARL: I wasn't yelling. I didn't...I thought you were still in the basement. You found it?

EDITH: I found a box.

PEARL: The box?

EDITH: A box. A box with papers.

PEARL: It's in there?

EDITH: I don't know, I haven't looked through it yet. It has father's writing, it says Edith and Pearl.

PEARL: Why do we have to bother with it?

EDITH: It's 75 dollars a month, of course it's worth it.

PEARL: Ferny Williams says she's not filling out the form... Doesn't want welfare.

EDITH: It's not welfare, it's Old Age Security.

PEARL: Maybe she doesn't want to be officially old.

EDITH: And she can afford not to take it. She had a husband with a good pension...and a son who can take care of her. We have no one.

PEARL: We have each other.

EDITH: Yes, but... "We" have no one.

PEARL: Want me to look?

EDITH: Please.

EDITH sits at the dining room table and starts to fill out the forms. PEARL starts searching, then stops.

PEARL: What am I looking for?

EDITH: A birth certificate.

PEARL: I don't remember ever seeing a birth certificate... Do we have to have a birth certificate?

EDITH: No, no they'll... Hmmm... *(Reading form.)* They'll accept baptismal certificates or even newspaper clippings of a birth announcement. Hmmm. Or a signed doctor's note.

PEARL: A doctor's note? Doctor Jenkins, if he were still alive, would be 133 years old.

EDITH: Something should be in there. Hmmm. It says here we have to fill out line 72...but there is no line 72, there is a box 72. I assume that's what they mean.

PEARL: Maybe it was thrown out.

EDITH: What have we ever thrown out? *(Pause.)* I'm filling in Box 72... I hope it's right. They say it'll take up to three months to process. If we fill it out wrong they'll send it back...and then it will take half a year before we'll get a cheque. Whatever the case, we should have something formal...some sort of identification.

PEARL: Why are they changing everything? I can't believe you voted for him.

EDITH: He spoke so well in the debate. And he's quite handsome.

PEARL: He's skinny and bald... Why does he want to know about us?

EDITH: I don't think Mr. Trudeau, personally, wants to know about us.

PEARL: I don't trust him.

EDITH: All the same... I was at the bank and the teller asked for my Social Insurance Number and I told her I didn't have one and she said you are supposed to have one, then she said she had to call the new manager and then we went through the whole thing again...and he says, Miss "Giddy" I need to know your SIN Number, and I said, "who keeps count." *(Chuckles.)*

PEARL: Hmmm.

EDITH: That was a joke, dear.

PEARL: Yes.

EDITH: Long and short of it we need a SIN Number. Hmmm...

PEARL: What?

EDITH: We could get a passport too.

PEARL: What would we do with a passport?

EDITH: You never know...maybe...hmmm...like that story in *Reader's Digest*.

PEARL: Which?

EDITH: That woman that found out she had three months to live? Sold everything and traveled around the world. She stayed in fancy hotels, ate in expensive restaurants, saw shows every night. Wouldn't that be something?

PEARL: She died after two months.

EDITH: She lived for two months. *(Pause.)* It would be good to have some identification.

PEARL finds something in the box.

PEARL: Hmmm.

EDITH: What is it?

PEARL: Nothing.

EDITH: Let me see.

PEARL hands her a small photo.

Ah, look at that. *(Pause.)* Is that you or me?

PEARL: I'm not sure.

EDITH: Look at that smile.

PEARL: It must be you.

EDITH writes a name on the back.

What are you doing? Don't put my name, we don't know it's me.

EDITH: It's you.

PEARL: No, no, put Pearl or Edith…

EDITH: It's you. You were a happy little baby.

PEARL: Humph.

EDITH: We don't have enough photos of you anyway.

She gives the photo back to PEARL.

PEARL: It's not me.

PEARL continues to look through the box. EDITH goes back to filling out the forms.

EDITH: *(Reading form.)* Line 78…? There is a line 78.

PEARL: Ahhh… What's this?

She hands a baptismal certificate to EDITH.

EDITH: Here we go. That's you. Now if we can find me.

PEARL: Where are you?

EDITH: I should be in there somewhere.

EDITH continues to fill out the form.

PEARL takes out a yellowed card.

She looks at it. She looks lost…

Of course if we get passports we'll need photographs taken. There is a place in Goderich… I could go in the next day or so. What do you think? Pearl dear?

She notices PEARL.

What do you have there? *(Pause.)* Pearl?

EDITH looks at the card.

Oh dear. *(Pause.)* Why would father have kept that? Let me have it.

PEARL does not move.

Pearl? Give me the invitation.

EDITH gently takes it from PEARL's hand. She looks at PEARL who is still frozen.

It should have been thrown away a long time ago.

EDITH takes the invitation and is about to throw it away.

PEARL: Don't.

EDITH: Pearl dear. *(Pause.)* Here, I'll put it in the box. I'll look and see if I can find me. *(She takes the box and starts to look through the papers.)* Must be in here somewhere… I'll find— Ahhh. Here I am. Good, good, now we can send them off.

EDITH puts the forms in the envelope. She sees PEARL is still lost in thought.

I just hope we filled it out right. What time is it?

EDITH looks at the clock on the wall that reads 7:05.

That clock's off again. *(Looks at her watch.)* Oh it's five past two. Where did the time go? We should straighten up before he comes.

PEARL: Before who comes?

EDITH: The boarder.

PEARL: What boarder?

EDITH: The boarder that is coming this afternoon

PEARL: We have a boarder coming?

EDITH: Any moment now.

PEARL: Did you tell me?

EDITH: I'm telling you now.

PEARL: Who is it?

EDITH: No one we know, but he's a friend of George's.

PEARL: Did you find out about him?

EDITH: Yes.

PEARL: What's his name?

EDITH: Hmmm.

PEARL: What's he do?

EDITH: (Do?)

PEARL: Where is he from?

EDITH: (Hmmm.)

PEARL: Do we know anything about him at all?

EDITH: He's a friend of George.

PEARL: Yes, you said that. I wouldn't call George a good judge of character.

EDITH: I thought you liked George.

PEARL: I do like George... But George likes everyone. Someone who likes everyone is by definition a bad judge of character. One should always dislike a few people.

EDITH: But Pearl, you dislike most people.

PEARL: And for good reason. *(Pause.)* We are letting a strange man into our home. Last year in Hespeler a man killed his landlady and chopped her into a hundred pieces. Edith, we are landladies!

EDITH: We will be careful.

PEARL: We have to be more than careful. We have to be... vigilant! Think of it...every time you read a book and there's a landlady, you know by the end she'll be murdered.

EDITH: Pearl.

PEARL: I clipped out an article from the *Kitchener Record*: Ten questions a landlady should ask her boarder. Or maybe it was fifteen questions.

EDITH: We've been taking in boarders for the last forty years and we've never had a problem.

PEARL: What about that salesman...the one that sold vacuum cleaners?

EDITH: That's why we ask for cash in advance.

PEARL: And that hippie.

EDITH: Michael.

PEARL: He played the piano when we were gone.

EDITH: We don't know that.

PEARL: I knew. I could tell. *(Pause.)* And he called us Pearl and Edith. He refused to call me Miss Gidley. He said he wouldn't participate in de-human… something— What was it?

EDITH: "Dehumanizing social structures."

PEARL: Yes! That's what it was. What does that even mean?

EDITH: Well it means…

PEARL: —That's right, you actually talked to him, I don't know how you could listen to him go on about it.

EDITH: It was quite interesting.

PEARL: He went on about how his generation was going to change the world. He couldn't even change his own socks.

There is a knock at the door.

EDITH: That's him.

PEARL stops and stares at the hallway to the front door.

It's alright Pearl. George said he was a nice boy. Shall we go to the door?

PEARL: It would look odd if we both met him at the door.

EDITH: Oh, I suppose… Do you want to—? *(Beat.)* Right! I'll go and meet him.

EDITH goes to the front door.

PEARL becomes quite agitated.

We hear the door opening.

PEARL retrieves the newspaper clipping "Fifteen Questions a Landlady Should Ask Her Boarder" from the drawer.

ANDREW: *(O.S.)* Good afternoon Miss Gidley.

EDITH: *(O.S.)* Afternoon… Where's George?

ANDREW: *(O.S.)* Oh, he had several other…deliveries. He had to make deliveries…

EDITH: *(O.S.)* And you are..?

ANDREW: *(O.S.)* Sorry?

EDITH: *(O.S.)* Your name. What is your name?

ANDREW: *(O.S.)* Oh— Charles.

EDITH: *(O.S.)* Ah Charles… Well, step in, step in…

ANDREW: *(O.S.)* Thank you Ma'am.

EDITH: *(O.S.)* Go on in.

ANDREW enters, he is pretty scruffy looking with longish hair and wearing jeans and a T-shirt. He is carrying an army duffle bag and a guitar case.

EDITH enters.

Ah, this is my sister Pearl.

ANDREW: Hello Miss Gidley… I'm Charles.

He reaches out to shake her hand, she does not.

PEARL: *(Pause.)* Hello.

EDITH: *(Pause.)* Well this is the living room.

EDITH exits to kitchen, ANDREW follows.

(O.S.) This is the kitchen, that door goes to the basement. Don't use the toaster and the kettle at the same time. The refrigerator door is fiddly, make sure it's closed properly.

They enter again.

The front door is for guests so use the side door, we generally use the side door. The bathroom is at the top of the stairs, end of the hall. You must be tired.

ANDREW: I've been on the road for a while.

EDITH: Let me show you to your room.

PEARL: First we have some questions for you.

EDITH: One or two.

PEARL: Fifteen.

ANDREW: Um… OK.

PEARL: I need to ask a few questions.

EDITH: That is if you don't mind.

ANDREW: That's fine. I'm hap—

PEARL: *(Reading from newspaper clipping.)* Name? What is your name?

ANDREW: Charles.

PEARL: *(Pause.)* Where are you from?

ANDREW: America.

PEARL: You're not being very specific.

ANDREW: Oh um… We—my family—were always travelin'. We were never in a place more than a year or two.

EDITH: Your father's a salesman?

ANDREW: No. He was in the army. That's why I've got an AB accent.

EDITH: AB accent?

ANDREW: Army Brat… As ABs you'd travel around so much that your accent sounds like "everywhere and nowhere".

EDITH: Well, you got to see the world.

ANDREW: Well, not the world, but got to see a lot of the states and…and a few countries.

EDITH: It must have been exciting.

ANDREW: Yeah… I guess.

EDITH: Seeing the world.

PEARL: How long are you intending to stay?

ANDREW: I don't know.

PEARL: You've no idea?

ANDREW: Um…no, not really. Ahh—

PEARL: Two days? *(Beat.)* Two years?

ANDREW: Oh, um two…maybe three days.

PEARL: Which?

ANDREW: Three.

PEARL: Three days.

ANDREW: Maybe longer— Is that a problem?

EDITH: No, that's not a problem.

PEARL: Where are you heading?

ANDREW: Heading?

PEARL: *(Reading from paper.)* "What is your intended destination?"

ANDREW: I don't know. I mean, I'm not going anywhere specific.

PEARL: *(Beat.)* Nowhere specific?

EDITH: All the young people today are traveling around,

seeing the country...seeing the world. It was different when we were young.

PEARL: What brings you to this area?

ANDREW: This area?

EDITH: I think it means what brings you to Ontario?

ANDREW: Oh um… *(Rehearsed sounding.)* I was in the army, I got injured, they sent me home and now I'm looking for a new life…Miss Gidley.

EDITH: Oh dear… injured?

ANDREW: I'm fine now… I mean I'm not… *(Pause.)* I'm fine.

PEARL: You were in the army?

ANDREW: Yes, Ma'am.

EDITH: Like your father. He must be proud of you.

ANDREW: Yes… *(Beat.)* he was.

EDITH: You were drafted?

ANDREW: No Ma'am! *(Beat.)* I enlisted.

EDITH: So you were over there?

ANDREW: Yes Ma'am.

EDITH: Vietnam. *(Pause.)* I see it on the news and I can't watch.

ANDREW: (Me neither.)

EDITH: Well Charles, I don't think we have any more questions.

PEARL: Yes we do.

EDITH: You look tired.

ANDREW: Yes Ma'am. I've been travelling for…several days and I only got a few hours' sleep.

EDITH: The room is at the top of the stairs to the left. You can unpack, freshen up, and maybe take a nap. Supper will be at six.

ANDREW: Thank you very much Miss Gidley, Miss Gidley.

EDITH: Charles, our names are Edith and Pearl.

ANDREW: I appreciate your hospitality Miss Pearl, Miss Edith.

ANDREW exits upstairs.

They watch in silence for a while.

PEARL: I had more questions.

EDITH: You asked enough questions.

PEARL: He said he was injured.

EDITH: Yes.

PEARL: He didn't look injured. When I asked where he was going he said "nowhere specific".

EDITH: Pearl dear.

PEARL: We don't even know his surname. We don't know anything about him.

EDITH: We know enough.

PEARL: He's hiding something from us.

EDITH: We're all hiding something.

PEARL: I had more questions. I bet you that woman in Hespeler didn't ask enough questions.

EDITH: Well, if he murders us in the night and chops us into a hundred little pieces, I'll make it up to you.

PEARL: Edith!

EDITH: We'll be fine.

PEARL: What if you're wrong about him?

EDITH: He called us Miss Pearl and Miss Edith.

PEARL: You just let him into our home without asking me.

EDITH: We need to make up the money from tuning the piano.

PEARL: *(Pause.)* Two days.

EDITH: (Only two?)

PEARL: He can stay for three days. No more.

EDITH: Good… Three days then. *(Pause.)* He's a good looking boy, no?

PEARL: I thought he looked rather scruffy. I suppose he'll be hungry.

EDITH: I bet you he hasn't had a decent home cooked meal in months. You should make your Sunday Roast.

PEARL: It's Tuesday.

EDITH: Yes… *(She quickly grabs her purse and jacket and goes to the door.)* I'll go to the Red and White and get a roast.

PEARL: Can we afford a roast? He's probably one of those big eaters. Remember that tall one?

EDITH: Tall one?

PEARL: The Dutch one… Vander-something.

EDITH: Oh yes! With the teeth, I've no idea where he put it all. We lost money just trying to feed him. I'll get a cheaper cut and we'll cook it a little longer.

EDITH is about to exit but sees PEARL lost in thought.

Pearl?

PEARL: *(She becomes aware of EDITH waiting.)* I can think can I not?

EDITH: I was just…

PEARL: Just go.

EDITH: I won't be long.

EDITH exits.

PEARL goes to the bottom of the stairs and looks up for a while.

Fade to black.

Sunday Dinner on Tuesday

Later that day. Evening.

EDITH is setting the dining room table for Sunday dinner for 6 people (or 4 people) White linen, fine china, silverware and even candles.

PEARL brings out some plates

PEARL: Your pumpkin pie looks odd.

EDITH: They were out of pumpkin so I used zucchini.

PEARL: Zucchini?

EDITH: Zucchini is a squash, pumpkin is a squash. Once you put in the cream and nutmeg you'll never notice the difference.

PEARL exits.

PEARL: *(O.S.)* It still looks odd.

EDITH: I'll put whipped cream on top.

EDITH exits.

ANDREW enters, looks at the table.

ANDREW: Hmmm.

He looks at his scruffy T-shirt and jeans.

Shit.

He thinks for a moment. He gets an idea, but then realizes its ramifications.

Shit.

He exits upstairs. EDITH enters, puts candles on the table. PEARL enters as EDITH lights the candles.

PEARL: Humph.

EDITH: You make the dinner, I get to set the table.

PEARL: I didn't say anything.

EDITH: You humph'd.

PEARL: Candles?

EDITH: I like candles.

PEARL: Everyone likes candles, but…

EDITH: What?

PEARL: It's a waste… You don't have to light them.

EDITH: We have a guest.

PEARL: He's not a guest, he's a boarder.

EDITH: Well, let him see them at least.

PEARL: I imagine he's seen candles before.

EDITH: Things are tight, but not that tight.

PEARL: But if we keep on wasting, things will be tight.

EDITH: Yes…we shouldn't waste money.

PEARL is about to blow them out and stops. She knows EDITH is alluding to the cost of tuning the piano.

Let's enjoy them for a few minutes. At least until grace.

PEARL: Until grace. *(Pause.)* Did you call him for dinner?

EDITH: Yes, several minutes ago. I thought I heard him come down.

PEARL: Obviously not.

EDITH: *(Yelling.)* CHARLES! Dinner's ready!

PEARL: Edith! You'd think this was a rooming house!

EDITH: I'm not going to climb the stairs twice.

PEARL: Hmmm?

EDITH: I already climbed the stairs and knocked on his door. I'm not going to do it again.

PEARL: But you needn't bellow.

EDITH: I'd rather wear out my voice than my knees. *(She hears something.)* Ahh. I'll give you a hand with the roast.

They exit to the kitchen.

ANDREW comes down the stairs.

He is wearing his uniform with tie. (He might have his hair slicked down).

He looks at himself in the mirror and sees his Bronze Star Medal.

He looks at the medal. He is clearly disturbed by it.

He tries to take the medal off but…

PEARL and EDITH enter carrying a roast and vegetables.

EDITH: *(Looking at ANDREW.)* My, my.

ANDREW: Sorry?

EDITH: Aren't we all gussied up.

ANDREW: It's the only good thing I own. I didn't even know it was Sunday.

PEARL: It's not.

ANDREW: Oh. It looks like Sunday dinner.

EDITH: It is.

ANDREW: Oh.

PEARL: Edith decided to have Sunday dinner on Tuesday.

ANDREW: 'Cause I…I didn't think it was Sunday… 'Course I didn't think it was Tuesday neither. I kinda lost track of…everything.

EDITH: Well. Have a seat, Charles.

ANDREW: Are there others coming?

EDITH: No, it's just the three of us.

ANDREW: Oh.

EDITH: The service has six settings. It looks better with six. Sit anywhere.

ANDREW goes to sit.

PEARL: Actually, *(Beat.)* I usually sit there.

ANDREW: Oh, sorry.

ANDREW moves toward another seat.

PEARL: Edith usually sits there. *(Beat.)* But anywhere else.

ANDREW tries to figure out where to sit.

Sit there. *(Gestures at third seat.)*

ANDREW sits down.

ANDREW: I haven't had a home cooked meal in…in months.

EDITH: Yes, we thought you might be hungry.

ANDREW: I am. Famished.

EDITH: Shall we?

EDITH folds her hands in prayer. She waits as ANDREW and PEARL fold their hands. She closes her eyes, and bows her head. PEARL and ANDREW do not.

Dearest Father. We are grateful for the bounty Thou hast given us and are truly thankful.

PEARL and ANDREW look at each other.

Bless this meal, and bless those less fortunate than we. And bless those who suffer,

ANDREW and PEARL see something in each other and look away.

…and bring them comfort. Amen.

ANDREW is lost in the moment.

PEARL stands and blows out one candle and goes to the other end of the table and blows out the other candle and then sits back down.

She notices ANDREW staring at her.

PEARL: It's a tradition.

EDITH: May I serve you?

ANDREW: Please. Miss Edith.

EDITH: What would you like?

ANDREW: As my grandpa used t'say. "Ever'thin' n' lots of it."

EDITH serves ANDREW.

EDITH: Well, it's nice when someone has an appetite. You'll need room for dessert.

ANDREW: It's a fine looking meal, Ma'am.

EDITH: Pearl did all the cooking.

ANDREW: A fine meal, Miss Pearl.

EDITH: I must say, Pearl, you out-did yourself.

PEARL: Don't forget about the rules.

EDITH: Yes, the rules. Almost forgot the rules.

PEARL: We have rules.

ANDREW: Yes Ma'am.

PEARL: You were in the army, so I imagine you know rules are everything.

ANDREW: I was quite good at following rules, Miss Pearl.

PEARL: Good, Mister Harken.

ANDREW is surprised she knows his name.

ANDREW: How'd you know my name?

PEARL: I can read. *(She points to his uniform.)*

ANDREW looks at his name tag.

ANDREW: Right.

PEARL: Good. So the rules: No female guests in the room at any time.

ANDREW: Yes Ma'am.

EDITH: We never used to have that rule.

PEARL: People would just assume that rule. But today with all that… What do they call it?

EDITH: Free love.

PEARL: Humph, free love.

ANDREW: Hmm hmmm.

PEARL: What?

ANDREW: Oh um… Well, it's just that I don't know anybody in town. I'd have a hard time breaking that rule.

EDITH: Oh I don't know, a uniform, medals… I imagine several of the women in town would—

PEARL: Rule number 2: This is not a restaurant.

ANDREW: Yes Ma'am.

EDITH: Dinner is at twelve thirty, supper at six, breakfast we fend for ourselves.

PEARL: If there is anything you don't like, let us know now. I'm not going to make a meal and not have it eaten.

ANDREW: Oh, I eat everything.

PEARL: No one eats everything.

ANDREW: Balut. (Bah-lute)

PEARL: Pardon me?

ANDREW: Balut. It's a delicacy from the Philippines.

EDITH: What is it?

ANDREW: Trust me, you don't want to know.

EDITH: You can't say that. Now I have to know.

ANDREW: Um... Well, it's a duck egg with the embryo inside...they boil it, and you eat it, beak and all.

EDITH: You're right, I didn't want to know.

ANDREW: I did warn you.

EDITH: Well, you're not a picky eater, that's good. We had a picky eater back—three fellows ago. There is something...I don't know...

PEARL: Selfish.

EDITH: Yes, that's it: picky eaters are selfish.

PEARL: Rule number three: You break something, you replace it. *(Pause.)* Rule number four: No alcohol in your room. Rule number five: Hmmm... What's rule number five?

EDITH: I can't remember.

PEARL: Whistling.

EDITH: Is it?

PEARL: Yes, remember? We had a whistler.

EDITH: He was friendly.

PEARL: Irritating man.

EDITH: Very good conversationalist.

PEARL: Tended to ramble. Which would be excusable, but that noise!

EDITH: True, he couldn't hold a tune. Well, no, it wasn't that. He just didn't whistle a tune. He just whistled.

No melody. Just notes. For hours on end. I think he was lonely.

PEARL: That incessant whistling drove away any friends he might've had.

EDITH: Maybe he was a widower…masking his grief.

PEARL: By causing it in others.

EDITH: He was well-read.

PEARL: Bit of a know-it-all.

EDITH: Pleasant smile.

PEARL: Edith fancied him.

EDITH: I did not…I just…I didn't mind him. I didn't even notice the whistling until Pearl brought it up. He was cultured, he was a theatre-goer But he said it with a capital T! "Theee-ah-taaah"! "Shall we go to the Theee-ah-taaah?"! Made it sound very grand. He took me to Stratford to see *Romeo and Juliet*. It was wonderful. I cried. I cried at the end, even though I knew what was going to happen…

PEARL: Because you knew what was going to happen. *(Pause.)* So, no whistling.

And where were we? What number?

EDITH: Six.

PEARL: Yes. Rule number six. *(Pause.)*

EDITH: *(Long pause.)* The piano should not be played. *(Beat.)* Touched!

Don't touch the piano… You don't have to say don't play it. *(Pause.)* The rule is: Do not touch the piano… *(Beat.)* unless-—

PEARL: There is no "unless"!

EDITH: *(Pause.)* Well…those are the rules.

ANDREW: It's beautiful.

PEARL: Hmm?

ANDREW: The piano, it's beautiful. A Bosendorfer?

EDITH: Yes… You know pianos?

ANDREW: Yeah, I used to play, took lessons for years. 'Course I never played a Bosendorfer. *(To PEARL.)* You play, Miss Pearl?

EDITH: *(Long pause.)* Pearl was a concert pianist.

ANDREW: Really? Wow. I'd love to hear you play…some time.

EDITH: Do you still play, Charles?

ANDREW: Nah, not really. It's probably like a bicycle. You never forget.

PEARL: Hmmm.

EDITH: But you play guitar?

ANDREW: Yes.

EDITH: Rock in Roll.

ANDREW: Yeah but it's, it's not "in" it's "and". Rock and roll.

EDITH: Rock and Roll.

ANDREW: Yeah, or Rock'n'roll.

EDITH: You said "in".

ANDREW: Not "in" but "nnn". Rock'n'roll.

EDITH: Rock'nnn'Roll.

ANDREW: Yeah, but I mostly play folk.

EDITH: We watched the "Beatles" on Ed Sullivan. All those girls screaming.

There is a knock at the side door.

After thirty seconds I felt like screaming myself.

There is another knock at the door.

I'll get the door, shall I?

EDITH goes to the door.

George?

GEORGE: Good evening Miss Gidley.

EDITH: Is everything alright?

GEORGE: Everything's fine.

EDITH: Oh.

GEORGE: I just have something in the car for Andr—

EDITH: Sorry?

GEORGE: Something *and* I wanted to give it to...him. I brought something for him.

EDITH: For Charles?

GEORGE: Yes, I have something for Charles.

EDITH: Ahh, have you eaten?

GEORGE: Oh no, no, I...I couldn't impose.

EDITH: Don't be silly. Have you eaten supper?

GEORGE: Yes, I had a tin of soup.

EDITH: That's not supper.

GEORGE: I'm full.

EDITH: Did you have dessert?

GEORGE: No.

EDITH: George, you must join us.

GEORGE: I do need to talk with Charles, for just a minute.

He enters and is surprised to see ANDREW in his uniform.

Charles?

ANDREW: Hello George.

GEORGE: Yes… Hello.

EDITH: Have a seat.

GEORGE doesn't sit. PEARL stands up and starts to clear the table.

(O.S.) Pumpkin pie, would everyone like pumpkin pie?

ANDREW: Yes, please.

GEORGE: Hmmm… You're…you're wearing your uniform.

ANDREW: Yeah.

GEORGE: *(Beat.)* Why?

ANDREW: It's the only good thing I own. We are having Sunday dinner.

GEORGE: It's Tuesday.

ANDREW: I know.

ANDREW and GEORGE watch PEARL exit with dishes.

What's wrong?

GEORGE: We've been raided.

ANDREW: What?

GEORGE: The RCMP have raided three safe houses.

ANDREW: What's going on?

GEORGE: They're looking for deserters.

ANDREW: Deserters?

PEARL comes back in.

PEARL: What was that?

ANDREW: Dessert. I was just telling George, I was looking forward to dessert.

PEARL: Ah.

ANDREW: Miss Pearl, that was a wonderful meal, thank you.

PEARL: It was Edith's idea.

EDITH: *(She pops her head in from kitchen.)* Would anyone like some coffee? I bought some special coffee, freeze dried instant.

ANDREW: Please.

GEORGE: Yes please, but um…

EDITH: Large mug, half full.

GEORGE: You remembered.

PEARL gathers up remaining plates. ANDREW and GEORGE watch her.

ANDREW: Do you need a hand?

PEARL: No, keep George company.

She exits.

ANDREW: Deserters?

GEORGE: Yeah.

ANDREW: But, I thought the police were leaving us alone.

GEORGE: Yeah, they're questioning everyone. They let the draft dodgers go. They're taking the deserters.

ANDREW: I don't understand. I didn't think they were deporting deserters.

GEORGE: I know, it doesn't make any sense…but what's really strange…

ANDREW: What?

GEORGE: They're saying something about a General.

ANDREW: A General?

GEORGE: I know, it doesn't make any sense, we'd know if a General had deserted. *(Pause.)* You alright?

ANDREW: Yeah…

GEORGE: You'll be safe here. You just need to lay low. Don't leave the house.

ANDREW: What?

GEORGE: It's a small town, word travels fast. No one knows you're here.

ANDREW: Except Miss Edith and Miss Pearl.

GEORGE: You told them your name was Charles. It's good they don't know your real name.

ANDREW: But they know my last name.

GEORGE: How?

ANDREW points to his name tag on his uniform.

That's not good… What about your story? Did you tell them what I told you?

ANDREW: Yeah, "I was in the army, I got injured, they sent me home, and now I'm looking for a new life."

GEORGE: Did they believe you?

ANDREW: Yeah, I think so... Why wouldn't they? It's the truth...kinda.

GEORGE: Yeah.

ANDREW: I feel like a politician.

GEORGE: What?

ANDREW: I tell them the truth, but they're hearing a lie.

GEORGE: Do you want them to know what you really are?

ANDREW: No.

GEORGE: Good, the less they know the better.

PEARL and EDITH enter with pie and coffee.

EDITH: Here you go.

GEORGE: Ahh. Pumpkin pie.

EDITH: It looks like the boys were talking while we were out of the room.

GEORGE: Politics.

EDITH: Don't get George talking about politics, he'll never stop.

GEORGE: A vibrant democracy is based on an informed public.

EDITH: See?

GEORGE: It's like the Social Insurance Number.

PEARL: What?

GEORGE: It's a way for the government to get control.

PEARL: *(To EDITH.)* I told you. Edith is trying to get us to fill out our forms.

EDITH: We are supposed to, it's the law.

GEORGE: We are no longer individuals, we are numbers. And as long as we are numbers the government can control us! Trudeau!

EDITH: I thought you would like Mr. Trudeau. He used to be NDP and before that he was a Communist.

GEORGE: And now he's a Liberal. See? He's moving to the right. Next he'll be a Conservative.

EDITH: George is our local protester. Last month he organized a March for Peace right down Queen Street.

GEORGE: We had a good turnout.

EDITH: How many people came?

GEORGE: Two hundred thousand in Washington, thirty thousand in Toronto.

EDITH: How many in town?

GEORGE: Twelve.

EDITH: Ahh.

GEORGE: It's a start.

EDITH: A very small start.

GEORGE: Twelve people can change the world. If people stood up five years ago America wouldn't be in this war. It's easy to start a war and almost impossible to end one. But we will! We will end this war. People will find out what is really going on. Nixon said they are there to liberate the country. Bombs don't liberate.

EDITH: I read that article in *Life* magazine...and that picture...a young boy in striped shirt and his sister running from... God knows what...and the fear on their little faces. I read that article three times and I still don't understand why they are in Vietnam.

ANDREW stands up.

ANDREW: Excuse me...I...I need to get some air.

He exits to the side porch.

EDITH: Did I...?

GEORGE: No, no it wasn't you. He's...

EDITH: Yes... right. I can't imagine what he must have gone through.

PEARL: *(Pause.)* George?

GEORGE: Right, I'll go have a chat with him.

GEORGE exits to the side porch.

We see PEARL and EDITH in the house in shadow.

GEORGE stands beside ANDREW.

You OK?

ANDREW: Yeah.

GEORGE: Really?

Pause.

What you are doing is right.

ANDREW: I don't know what I'm doing here.

GEORGE: Who does?

ANDREW: I'm not a peacenik or nothin'... I'm just...I don't know, I'm... *(Pause.)* I don't know.

GEORGE: You'll figure it out

ANDREW: A few months ago I would have spat on someone like me. And now…? And now…?

GEORGE: *(Pause.)* Hear that?

ANDREW: What?

GEORGE: Listen. *(Pause.)* Crickets.

ANDREW: *(He listens for a moment.)* I don't hear nothin'.

GEORGE: That's 'cause they're not chirping. You can tell winter is coming 'cause the crickets stop chirping.

ANDREW: Really?

GEORGE: You know what happens to them?

ANDREW: No.

GEORGE: I always wondered. I thought they were hibernating or something. So I went to the library to find out. Turns out, they freeze to death. They gotta lay their eggs in the ground before they die. All that chirping? It's just to attract mates so they can lay as many eggs as possible before they freeze to death.

ANDREW: Oh. *(Pause.)* Hmmm *(Pause.)* I'm…I'm sorry but I, I don't quite understand the analogy.

GEORGE: When I'm feeling really bad I think, "Thank God I'm not a cricket."

ANDREW laughs.

What you are doing is right…in ways you'll never understand.

ANDREW: Well…

GEORGE: You want to talk about what happened?

ANDREW: *(He is about to say yes but…)* (No.)

GEORGE: *(Pause.)* 'Kay. *(Pause.)* I'll drop by in a day or two… Call me if you notice anything.

ANDREW: Yeah. Thanks for… *(Beat.)* Thanks.

GEORGE: Tell the Gidley girls thanks for dessert.

ANDREW: You only had a bite.

GEORGE: Yeah. That's the worst pumpkin pie I've ever tasted. Goodnight Andrew.

ANDREW: Charles.

GEORGE: Charles. Sorry. Charles. *(Pause.)* Goodnight Charles.

ANDREW: Goodnight George.

GEORGE exits.

GEORGE: *(O.S.)* Don't worry, everything will be fine.

ANDREW: Unless you're a cricket.

ANDREW looks down at his jacket. He sees the medal. He grabs his medal and rips it off. He looks at it.

Fade to black.

Act II

The Medal

It is ten o'clock the next morning.

PEARL is standing in the living room holding ANDREW's medal. She is thinking.

EDITH comes down the stairs.

EDITH: *(Whispering.)* I think he's still sleeping.

PEARL still looks at medal.

(Whispering.) Pearl dear? *(Pause.)* Pearl?

PEARL: Hmmm?

EDITH: *(Whispering.)* I said – *(Sees medal.)* What's that?

PEARL: A medal.

EDITH: Charles'?

PEARL: Yes.

EDITH: Where was it?

PEARL: Outside. *(Points to the porch.)*

EDITH: Outside?

PEARL: Yes.

EDITH: Why would he—? *(Pause.)* Oh.

PEARL: What?

EDITH: Nothing.

PEARL: That "oh" wasn't a nothing.

EDITH: I'm not sure…

PEARL: What do you know?

EDITH: I know as much as you do.

PEARL: We don't know anything, because you didn't let me ask enough questions.

EDITH: We know enough.

PEARL: Why would he throw his medal away?

EDITH: We don't know he threw it away, maybe he dropped it.

PEARL: It wasn't dropped.

PEARL shows EDITH the medal, the clasp is twisted and there is some material on the pin.

Where is he?

EDITH: I told— He's still in his room.

PEARl: Sleeping?

EDITH: Yes.

PEARL: He should have been up hours ago.

EDITH: Maybe he's on a different time.

PEARL: Sleeping his life away.

EDITH: He looked tired.

PEARL: Hmmm… *(Pause.)* What should we do with it?

EDITH: Put it back where you found it.

PEARL: I'm not throwing it back outside.

EDITH: Well, you can't give it back to him.

PEARL: I'll keep it.

EDITH: What if he wants to…? What if he wants it back?

PEARL: I'll ask him.

EDITH: No! Just put it back.

PEARL: I'm keeping it

PEARL puts the medal in a drawer.

EDITH exits to the kitchen.

PEARL takes out an ancient upright vacuum cleaner, plugs it in and is about to turn it on…

EDITH comes out with a casserole dish.

EDITH: I should— What are you doing?

PEARL: I'm going to vacuum.

EDITH: It's making that horrible squealing sound… You don't want to wake him.

PEARL: It's after ten.

EDITH: Let him sleep. He looked so tired. I'll do it when I get back.

PEARL: Get back?

EDITH: It's Wednesday. Shut-ins.

PEARL: In Goderich?

EDITH: Yes.

PEARL: You're still going?

EDITH: Yes.

PEARL: We have a boarder.

EDITH: We don't both need to be here.

PEARL: I heard sounds.

EDITH: Sounds?

PEARL: Yes, last night, from his room.

EDITH: I didn't hear anything.

PEARL: You can sleep through a thunderstorm. Yelling, he was yelling and banging things.

EDITH: Poor boy.

PEARL: Darlene said Thomas had soldier's heart for years after he came back.

EDITH: That was an accident.

PEARL: Drown in that creek by accident?

EDITH: *(Looking upstairs.)* Charles wouldn't... He's not... He's not like Thomas.

Let him sleep. I'll vacuum when I get back. I won't be long.

PEARL: You don't have to go.

EDITH: He's expecting me.

EDITH starts to exit.

PEARL: The other ladies can take it to him.

EDITH stops.

EDITH: *(Pause.)* There are no others.

PEARL: What?

EDITH: It's just me.

PEARL: Why would it just be you—? *(Pause.)* Why aren't the

other women going with you? *(Pause.)* Edith? Who is it? *(Pause.)* Who is it Edith?

EDITH: *(Pause.)* John Maison.

PEARL: John Maison?

EDITH: Yes.

PEARL: Of all people.

EDITH: His wife passed away…he has no one.

PEARL: And now he's a shut-in. I suppose there is some justice in the world. How much time does he have left?

EDITH: Who knows…

PEARL: Edith?

EDITH: Yes? *(Pause.)* He's not a shut-in, he's not sick. He's just… He's just lonely.

PEARL: That man should be alone for the rest of his life for what he did to you.

EDITH: *(Pause.)* I'm going.

PEARL: But…

EDITH: He's expecting me. *(Pause.)* I'll be back late.

EDITH goes to exit out the front door.

PEARL: Edith! Think about what you are doing.

EDITH stops and looks at PEARL.

EDITH comes back into the room.

PEARL lightens and smiles.

Good.

EDITH continues to look at PEARL.

You should be careful… People don't change.

EDITH is about to say something but stops herself.

EDITH: *(Pause.)* I'll be back later. Have supper without me.

EDITH exits.

PEARL: EDITH! Edith! *(Pause.)* …Edith.

PEARL is lost. PEARL looks up the stairs. She climbs two stairs and stops.

She turns on the vacuum cleaner. It squeals and drones. It is very loud.

She lets it run without moving it.

PEARL hears ANDREW coming down the stairs and starts to actually vacuum.

ANDREW: Good morning!

PEARL: SORRY?

ANDREW: I said, GOOD MORNING!

She shuts off the vacuum cleaner.

Good morning.

PEARL: Sorry, did I wake you?

ANDREW: No, it's fine.

PEARL: I can vacuum later if it bothers you.

ANDREW: No Ma'am.

PEARL: Good.

ANDREW: I'm just going to have some breakfast.

ANDREW exits to the kitchen and enters with a bowl and spoon, box of cereal and a carton of milk.

He is about to pour the cereal when PEARL moves.

PEARL takes the cereal, bowl, spoon, and milk away from him and goes toward the kitchen and stops.

PEARL: Morning's over.

ANDREW: Oh.

PEARL: It's after ten.

ANDREW: Oh.

PEARL: Breakfast is any time in the morning. *(Pause.)* Morning being any time between six and eight… maybe eight-thirty.

ANDREW: Oh, I didn't know.

PEARL: Yes, one assumes.

She exits with his breakfast.

PEARL returns to the room.

ANDREW still sits at the table.

We have rules.

ANDREW: Yes Ma'am.

There is an uncomfortable pause.

PEARL: I suppose we were not clear about the rules. Ten o'clock is mid-morning, not morning.

ANDREW: Right.

PEARL: *(Pause.)* We can't just go and change the rules!

ANDREW: Right.

PEARL: We can't…we can't just change everything.

ANDREW: I understand Ma'am.

PEARL is about to say something and stops herself.

She sits down at the table across from ANDREW.

She endeavours to make light conversation.

PEARL: *(Pause.)* You're a late sleeper?

ANDREW: No.

PEARL: Oh.

ANDREW: I don't usually sleep in. *(Beat.)* I don't usually sleep.

PEARL: You've been…travelling. Edith thought you might be on a different time.

ANDREW: Yeah… Yeah, I'm on a different time. Where is Miss Edith?

Pause.

Miss Pearl? *(Pause.)* Are you alright?

PEARL: *(Pause.)* What?

ANDREW: Are you alright?

PEARL: *(Pause.)* Um…

ANDREW: Ma'am, is there…?

PEARL: She's gone to see him.

ANDREW: Oh.

PEARL: Why would she do that?

ANDREW: I don't know.

PEARL: As if she's forgotten…

ANDREW: Who?

PEARL: She had come back to be with me. Because... because that's what sisters do, is it not?

ANDREW: Yeah.

PEARL: Then he left her! Didn't give a reason.

ANDREW: I'm sorry.

PEARL: So we took care of each other, we did. *(Pause.)* Coward!

ANDREW: What?

PEARL: Refused to leave town. He...he, stayed and tormented her. What kind of man does that?

ANDREW: Um...

PEARL goes to the front door.

PEARL: I should have stopped her! Should have taken care of her! She should be back... *(She looks at the clock.)* Is it so late?

ANDREW: It's just after ten.

PEARL: Is it?

She looks at ANDREW.

This house won't clean itself.

PEARL starts to vacuum. It squeals loudly.

ANDREW: Miss PEARL!

PEARL: YES?

ANDREW: Your belt's loose!

She turns off vacuum.

PEARL: Sorry?

ANDREW: Your belt's loose. That's what makes that noise.

PEARL: Oh.

ANDREW: It just needs to be tightened. There's usually a screw that can be adjusted.

ANDREW takes the vacuum and tips it back.

PEARL: Don't break it.

ANDREW: It's already kinda broken. The squealing sound is the belt slipping. It's hard on the motor and hard on the belt. It'll only get worse.

He looks at the bottom of the vacuum.

Ahh! That looks like it.

PEARL: Do you need some tools? We have tools.

ANDREW reaches into his pocket.

ANDREW: No thanks, I can do it with a dime. *(To himself.)* Righty tighty.

PEARL: What was that?

ANDREW: That should do it.

He puts the vacuum back and turns it on; it is quiet.

PEARL: Well.

ANDREW: You can continue vacuuming.

PEARL shuts it off.

PEARL: Thank you Charles. You must be hungry.

ANDREW: Yes, I am.

PEARL: Make sure you don't miss dinner.

ANDREW: *(Pause.)* Right. *(Pause.)* Twelve-thirty?

PEARL: Yes, twelve-thirty.

ANDREW: Well then…

ANDREW exits upstairs.

PEARL watches him leave. She then continues to vacuum area rug in front of the piano.

PEARL stops and looks at the piano. She puts away the vacuum cleaner.

She picks up a dust rag and liquid furniture polish.

She pours furniture polish on the rag and starts to dust the piano.

PEARL puts more and more passion in the dusting.

ANDREW comes down with the guitar. He watches her for a moment.

He goes outside and takes out his guitar and a song book.

PEARL hears the sound of a guitar being quickly tuned and then strummed.

PEARL turns on the radio to a news program.

She can still hear the music.

She turns it up louder.

She can still hear the music.

She tunes the radio to static between two stations and turns it up louder.

The cacophony of sound increases.

Fade to black.

Where is Edith?

It is evening, eith o'clock. It is dark out.

ANDREW is still on the porch. It is clear that he has spent a good part of the day there.

PEARL is sitting in her chair, clearly worried. She gets up and looks out the window.

ANDREW starts playing again.

PEARL goes to the side door.

PEARL: Can you stop playing!

ANDREW stops playing.

PEARL goes back to her chair.

ANDREW enters the house puts the guitar against the wall and looks at PEARL.

She's not back yet.

ANDREW: I'm sure she's fine.

PEARL: Fine? What do you know?

ANDREW: Well um…

PEARL: I know where she is.

ANDREW: Have you tried calling there?

PEARL: I'm not talking to that man.

ANDREW: I'm sure she'll be back soon.

PEARL: *(Pause.)* She's never late. And it's already— (*Looks at clock.*)

ANDREW: It's almost eight.

PEARL: That stupid clock. It's always wrong! I should

have thrown it away a long time ago. That, that... stupid...stupid clock!

ANDREW: Maybe it can be fixed.

PEARL: We've had it for years, we haven't fixed it yet. We can't afford to fix it.

ANDREW: Maybe I could have a look.

PEARL: You fix vacuum cleaners and clocks?

ANDREW: I've never fixed a clock, but there's only so many things it could be. *(Pause.)* It's mechanical, so either something loose, something stiff, something cracked, or something missing.

PEARL: So, there are only four things that could be wrong?

ANDREW: No, it's more like one of a thousand things wrong, but only four categories of broken.

He puts the clock on the table.

PEARL: Do you even know what you're doing?

ANDREW: Not really. But I can at least try.

He looks at the clock.

I'll need some tools. I don't think I can fix this with a dime.

PEARL: Father's tool shed. Out back.

ANDREW: I'll see what I can do.

PEARL: If you want real tools, you should talk to George.

ANDREW: George has good tools, does he?

PEARL: Of course.

ANDREW: Right.

PEARL: For his work.

ANDREW: Yeah.

PEARL: You don't know what George does?

ANDREW: He's more of a… He's a friend of a friend.

PEARL: George is a piano tuner.

ANDREW: Really? *(Beat.)* I'll see what I can find in the shed.

He exits to the shed.

PEARL thinks for a moment.

She picks up phone and holds it for a moment trying to build up courage to call.

She dials "0".

PEARL: Hello, Operator? Yes I'd like to make a long distance call to Goderich. *(Pause.)* Mr. John Maison. *(Pause.)* Maison! With an "I" *(Pause.)* M-A-I-S-O-N *(Pause.)* well I don't know his address— Goderich *(Pause.)* Thank you. *(Pause.)* Could you make that a collect call? *(Pause.)* Miss Pearl Gidley…. G-I-D-L-E-Y *(Pause.)* Thank you. *(She listens to it ring several times.)* Hello? (Pause.) No, Operator, let it ring a few more times.

She listens to the phone ring and then hears a car arriving.

PEARL hangs up phone.

She is relieved as she hears EDITH arrive and then hardens as she hears the door open. She goes back to her chair.

EDITH enters carrying a casserole dish and wicker shopping basket.

She sees PEARL. EDITH smiles.

EDITH: Hello Pearl.

PEARL does not answer.

EDITH puts the basket on the table.

I said, "Hello" Pearl. *(Pause.)* I know, I'm late. It took longer than I thought it would. I did say I might be late. I hope you weren't worried.

Well, I bought some more tea…Ceylon. Would you like some?

Takes out a tin of Twining's tea from the basket.

Look at that, it says the Queen of England herself drinks it. I'll make us a pot, hmmm? *(Pause.)* Maybe later.

EDITH exits.

We hear the sound of EDITH filling up a vase.

I had to run some errands. I took our forms to the office in London. It's faster if you go in person, even though we had to wait in line for an hour.

She enters with vase of water.

I barely recognized the city, London, everything has changed. We should go there…it's been ages since we've been there. We'll go to Eaton's, so much better than looking through a catalogue.

EDITH takes out a bouquet of flowers from the basket.

PEARL: Humph.

EDITH: They're for you.

EDITH starts carefully arranging the flowers into the vase.

PEARL watches for a moment and then…

PEARL: They're pretty. *(Pause.)* Thank you Edee.

EDITH continues to arrange the flowers.

EDITH: They're from him.

PEARL: I don't want them.

EDITH: John's just being nice.

PEARL: Nice? What does he want?

EDITH: *(Pause.)* He wants me to be happy.

PEARL: By giving me flowers?

EDITH: Yes.

PEARL: See what he's doing? He'll leave you and—

EDITH continues to arrange the flowers.

EDITH: He is leaving. Next week.

PEARL: —I told you, see—

EDITH: —For three months. Like the story.

PEARL: What story?

EDITH: In *Reader's Digest*. I read him that story. He said, "Why wait to be told you are going to die before you decide to live." He's taking the life insurance money to travel around the world.

PEARL: What a foolish man.

EDITH: He asked me to join him. I told him no.

PEARL: What on earth was he thinking?

EDITH: I said to him what would people think, two single people traveling together? He said, "At our age, they'd think we were married." And then he blushed. So I said yes.

PEARL: What?

EDITH: Yes. I said "yes".

PEARL: After what he did to you? What makes you think he's changed?

EDITH: He hasn't changed!

PEARL: Edith?

EDITH: He… He didn't leave me! I left him!

PEARL: You told me that he left you!

EDITH: No, I said nothing! NOTHING! You assumed!

PEARL: What did he do…? …to make you leave?

Pause.

Why did you leave?

There is a knock at the door.

Pause.

Why did you leave him?

There is another knock.

EDITH: There's someone at the door.

PEARL: Edith?

EDITH goes to the side door.

GEORGE is there.

EDITH: George?

GEORGE: Hello, Miss Gidley.

EDITH: Is everything alright?

GEORGE: Yes, Miss Gidley.

There is an uncomfortable pause.

May I come in?

EDITH: What? *(Beat.)* Oh yes, of course, come in George.

GEORGE enters looking for ANDREW and sees PEARL.

GEORGE: Hello Miss G—

PEARL: What's wrong?

GEORGE: Nothing…nothing's wrong.

PEARL: Then what do you want?

GEORGE: Did I come at a bad time?

PEARL: Yes.

GEORGE: Oh…

EDITH: Pearl!

PEARL: You're here now. What do you want?

GEORGE: Um…

EDITH: Pearl! George I'm sorry.

PEARL: Edith! Don't apologize for me! What do you want George?

GEORGE: Um…Charles, I need to talk to Charles.

PEARL: What about?

GEORGE: I need to… Is he here? I need to talk to him.

PEARL: What about?

EDITH: Well, if it's a private matter between George and Charles, then it's none of our business.

PEARL: Well, if it's none of our business, just tell us: Miss Pearl, it's none of your business!

GEORGE: Um.

EDITH: I'll get him for you George. Charles?! George wants to see you! Charles?!

EDITH starts to climb the stairs.

PEARL: Don't wear out your knees, he's not up there.

EDITH: Then where is he?

PEARL: He went out.

GEORGE: What?

PEARL: He went out.

GEORGE: Where'd he go?

PEARL: What's wrong George?

GEORGE: Nothing.

PEARL: George, it seems like there is something wrong.

GEORGE: I need to find him.

EDITH: Pearl, why did he leave?

PEARL: He said he was going to fix something, and then he left.

GEORGE: Oh no.

EDITH: Did he say when he was coming back?

PEARL: No, he didn't.

GEORGE: This is bad, this is really bad. If they find him…

PEARL: If who finds him?

GEORGE: *(Pause.)* Um.

PEARL: Who is looking for Charles? *(Pause.)* George?

GEORGE: Yes?

PEARL: Who is looking for Charles?

GEORGE: *(Pause.)* The RCMP.

EDITH: Oh dear lord! What has he done?

GEORGE: He hasn't done anything.

PEARL: Then why is the RCMP looking for him?

ANDREW enters with a tool box.

ANDREW: I found the tool box. Your father had very nice tools. I— Ah, Miss Edith, you're back, you had us worried. *(He sees GEORGE.)* George?

They all look at ANDREW

(Pause.) Is something wrong?

EDITH/PEARL /GEORGE: Yes.

ANDREW: Oh.

PEARL: The RCMP is looking for you.

ANDREW: Me?

PEARL: What did you do?

ANDREW: I… I…

PEARL: Why is the RCMP looking for you?

ANDREW: Um…George?

GEORGE: Your father…

ANDREW: My father?

GEORGE: Your father is General Harken?

ANDREW: Yeah, but-—

GEORGE: He's the reason they are looking for you.

ANDREW: But, I'm in Canada.

GEORGE: Your father must know someone.

ANDREW: God, I should have known he'd— I don't understand how…?

GEORGE: The RCMP are picking them up and taking them across the border and handing them to the FBI.

PEARL: The FBI? The RCMP? What have you done?

GEORGE: He didn't do anything wrong. He's innocen—

PEARL: The RCMP doesn't go after innocent people! Charles? What have you done?

ANDREW doesn't answer.

You must have done something, something terrible! I just want the truth! Can someone please tell me the goddamn truth?

ANDREW: I'm… *(Pause.)* I'm a deserter.

EDITH: Oh dear.

PEARL: A deserter?

ANDREW: Yes Ma'am.

PEARL: Do you actually think we would want a deserter, a coward…? …living in my home?!

ANDREW: No Ma'am…probably not.

EDITH: Yes we would.

PEARL: Edith?

EDITH: I've been happy to have a deserter living in my home.

PEARL: You knew?

EDITH: Yes.

PEARL: But you said nothing. That's why you didn't want me to ask any more questions. You didn't want me to know the truth. Why have you been keeping the truth from me?

EDITH: Because you…

PEARL: Because I what? *(Pause.)* What ?

PEARL goes to exit then stops. She slowly goes to EDITH.

Why did you leave him?

Why did you leave John? *(Pause.)* Tell me!

EDITH: To take care of you.

PEARL: You didn't need to take care of me!

EDITH: Of course I needed to! Who would have taken care of you when you tried to… (end it all).

PEARL: I never would have done that!

EDITH : But you did! You stopped living! You…you… stopped! Someone had to take care of you.

PEARL: You should have told me! If I had known, I would have never, never let you stay!

EDITH: I know, (that's why I did it.)

PEARL : *(Quietly.)* You lied. You all…lied.

PEARL exits.

GEORGE: I shouldn't have never brought Charles here, I'm sorry.

EDITH: No, it wasn't you. It started long ago…

GEORGE: *(Pause.)* You should pack up, get ready to go. I'll be back first thing tomorrow morning. It's not safe to stay with me. I'll have to find a new place. If your father gets his way, they'll send you to prison.

ANDREW: Prison?

GEORGE: That's what you'll get if they find you.

EDITH: Your father would do that to you?

ANDREW: Yes. *(Pause.)* Yeah, I guess he would.

EDITH: His own son?

ANDREW: My father is a man of principles. The army is his life, I'm a distant second on that list. And now that I've betrayed my country…well…that's just unforgivable.

GEORGE: Fathers and sons. *(Pause.)* You're lucky, my father left the minute he set eyes on me. I never got a chance to disappoint him.

ANDREW: Hmmm.

GEORGE: *(To EDITH.)* Miss Pearl?

EDITH: She'll be… *(Pause.)* I'll take care of her, George.

GEORGE goes to side door and looks to the sky.

GEORGE: Storm's coming.

EDITH: How can you tell?

GEORGE: Heard it on the radio. Goodnight Miss Edith… Andrew.

GEORGE exits.

EDITH: Andrew? Your name is Andrew?

ANDREW: Yes, yes it is.

EDITH: It doesn't suit you.

ANDREW: I was getting used to Charles.

EDITH: Yes. (So am I.)

ANDREW: You knew all along?

EDITH: Hmm?

ANDREW: That I was a deserter?

EDITH: I wasn't certain, but…yes.

ANDREW: Thank you.

EDITH: *(Pause.)* Poor John. She told you that he left me?

ANDREW: Yeah.

EDITH: Hmm…I should have told her the truth.

ANDREW: You left him to take care of Miss Pearl?

EDITH: Yes— *(Pause.)* Don't look at me like that, I'm not a saint, it's what we did back then, we… we took care of each other. *(Pause.)* It's what we did. *(Pause.)* It's what we do.

ANDREW: What happened to Miss Pearl?

EDITH: *(Pause.)* It's late. *(Pause.)* You look tired, get some sleep.

ANDREW: Yeah…I don't usually sleep…really. I'm just gonna… Gonna wait for George.

He picks up the clock.

EDITH: You're going to fix the clock?

ANDREW: Probably not, but I'll try…I'll probably make it worse.

EDITH: It's a clock that doesn't tell time, how much worse can it be? Goodnight.

ANDREW: Goodnight Miss Edith.

EDITH exits. ANDREW starts to work on the clock. He takes out a screwdriver.

Lefty loosey.

There is a rumble of thunder. ANDREW goes to window. Another rumble of thunder. He looks out.

Fade to black.

The Storm

Fade up the sound of a storm. Wind blowing, rain falling, branches banging against the house.

ANDREW is asleep on the couch. The clock and tools are in front of him on the coffee table.

The sound of a rainstorm outside increases, there is the rumble of thunder.

ANDREW is moaning in his sleep.

ANDREW: *(Still sleeping.)* Stop... No... (Vietnamese) Dung lai.... Dung lai. (Stop)

PEARL comes down the stairs and slowly makes her way to ANDREW. ANDREW moans.

(Vietnamese) Gio tay. (Hands up!) Mmmm. Mmmmm. Nam xuong! (Lie down!)

ANDREW moans again.

PEARL leans over him. She takes a throw that is on a chair and lays it over ANDREW. ANDREW startles awake, and grabs PEARL's arm.

Identify yourself or I'll break your fucking neck.

PEARL: Ahhhh!

ANDREW is shocked but still disoriented. He lets go of her arm.

ANDREW: There was a…

He runs to the window and looks out.

There was…I was…I was…

PEARL: Charles!

ANDREW: Miss Pearl?

PEARL: You were having a nightmare!

ANDREW: Oh God! I'm sorry I… I…

PEARL starts to move and then wobbles.

PEARL: Oh my…I need to sit down.

He helps her to her chair.

ANDREW: Here you go Ma'am.

PEARL: *(Pause.)* Oh dear…

ANDREW: What is it?

PEARL: My heart's racing.

ANDREW: You alright?

PEARL: Yes, yes…I'll…I'll just sit here for a moment.

ANDREW: Can I, can I, get you someth—

PEARL: No, no…I'm just out of…out of breath.

ANDREW sits down on the armchair.

ANDREW: It's the adrenaline…you had an adrenaline rush.

PEARL: Oh my… Oh dear… How long will this last?

ANDREW: A long time.

PEARL: Oh?

ANDREW: But…yeah…that was when the V.C. were trying to kill us.

PEARL: Really?

ANDREW: Maybe several minutes.

PEARL: Well then…

ANDREW: *(Pause.)* Miss Pearl? When I woke up… I…um… *(Pause.)* I'm sorry for what I said.

PEARL: What are you talking about?

ANDREW: When I…as I woke up I, I said…I said—

PEARL: You were mumbling, couldn't make out a thing.

ANDREW: Oh.

PEARL: I should go back to bed…

She starts to stand.

Ooooh.

ANDREW: No, you shouldn't move, just…just stay here.

PEARL: I'll be fine.

ANDREW: Please, Miss Pearl. You should sit for a while. You're lucky, an adrenaline rush at your age…

PEARL: *(Pause.)* What? *(Pause.)* It could have killed me?

ANDREW: *(Pause.)* Yeah, I'm—

PEARL: Really? *(Pause.)* Well, that would have complicated things for you, wouldn't it?

ANDREW: Sorry? *(Pause.)* You should, you should drink some water. I'll get you a glass.

PEARL: I'm not thirsty.

ANDREW: You will be, trust me… You really should drink.

ANDREW exits.

PEARL sees the clock on the coffee table.

PEARL: Hmmm.

PEARL looks at her knees. She slowly stands up and starts moving them.

Well I'll be…

ANDREW enters with the water.

ANDREW: Here you go Miss Pearl. *(Hands her the glass of water.)*

PEARL: I can't feel my legs.

ANDREW: Oh God! Maybe we should take you to the hospital.

PEARL: No, I, I can feel them, but…but, I can't feel the pain. They've been hurting since…forever. The pain's gone. I feel…. *(She can't find the words.)*

ANDREW: It's the adrenaline.

PEARL: Really?

ANDREW: Yeah. It's powerful stuff. When I was shot, it took me twenty minutes before I felt the pain.

PEARL: You really were shot?

ANDREW: Yeah. *(Pause.)* Went through my side. Sounds worse than it is. Doctor said I was lucky, bullet missed everything…well, everything except for me.

PEARL: Sorry I—

ANDREW: Yeah. They say an adrenaline rush is closest we

come to being superhuman. You could pick up a 250-pound guy like he weighed nothin'...or react without even... Without even thinking. *(Realizing.)* I wasn't mumbling when I woke up, was I? *(Pause.)* I'm sorry for what I said.

PEARL: It's not as if I've never heard that word before. *(Pause.)* But, this was the first time it was directed at me.

ANDREW laughs.

(Pause.) What happened? Over there... What happened?

ANDREW: *(Pause.)* He was just a kid...twelve, maybe thirteen... But according to the army, he wasn't a kid, he was shooting at us, killed two of our men, he was an enemy combatant. So... *(Pause.)* they gave me a medal. He was just a kid.

PEARL: Oh dear...

ANDREW: I betrayed everything I ever believed in, and they... If they'd done anything, anything but...a medal. I didn't deserve a medal for what I did.

PEARL: No, you didn't deserve that medal. *(She looks at him till he realizes.)* It doesn't belong to you... So return it.

ANDREW: (What?)

PEARL: Return the medal.

ANDREW: (Return it?)

PEARL: You can give it back.

ANDREW: I can't (I threw it away).

PEARL looks at ANDREW and then hears something.

PEARL: *(Pause.)* Do you hear that?

ANDREW: What?

PEARL: The dripping from the eavestrough…like a little tune.

ANDREW: Yeah, your hearing becomes acute.

PEARL: Isn't that something.

ANDREW: Yeah.

PEARL: They should put that in a pill.

ANDREW: They do.

PEARL: *(Pause.)* Well, no use going back to bed. I'm wide awake. Breakfast, I think I'll make us some breakfast.

ANDREW: You should still rest.

PEARL: My knees aren't hurting, I can hear everything and I feel twenty years younger. I'm not going to waste that sitting down. You want some too?

ANDREW: I should get ready to go.

PEARL: Go?

ANDREW: Yes.

PEARL: You're not leaving 'till you fix that clock. Rule number three: You break something, you fix it.

ANDREW: *(Beat.)* Right.

PEARl: I feel like making scones. Would you like some scones?

ANDREW: That would be wonderful, Miss Pearl.

PEARL: Good.

ANDREW: What are scones?

PEARL: They're like a biscuit.

ANDREW: Oh, that would be great.

PEARL exits.

ANDREW looks at the clock and opens up the back.

PEARL enters.

PEARL: Raisins or currants?

ANDREW: Ah!

PEARL: What?

ANDREW: It's really dusty.

PEARL: Sorry.

ANDREW: No, that's good. Dust makes it stiff, it might just take a good cleaning.

He brushes off the dust with a small paint brush.

It's probably still unf— Ah!

PEARL: What?

ANDREW: It ticked…

PEARL: It's working?

ANDREW: No. But… *(Fiddles with something.)* Ah. Another tick.

He fiddles a bit more.

PEARL: Shouldn't it tock?

ANDREW: Hmm?

PEARL: Tock? Tick tock.

ANDREW laughs.

ANDREW: Yeah, yeah it should tock. Maybe that's what is wrong with it. I'll see if I can get it to tock.

She sees something in ANDREW.

PEARL: What is it?

ANDREW: The medal? I threw it away and it didn't make me feel any better.

PEARL: I know.

ANDREW: (What do you mean?)

PEARL takes the medal from the drawer.

PEARL: You didn't betray your country, your country betrayed you. It wasn't your fault.

She hands ANDREW the medal.

It doesn't belong to you…return it.

ANDREW looks at the medal.

ANDREW: Miss Pearl?

PEARL: You can give it back.

ANDREW: *(Pause.)* Thank you.

PEARL: Raisins or currants?

ANDREW: *(Pause.)* Currants, please Ma'am.

PEARL goes to the kitchen.

PEARL: You should ask George…about returning the medal.

PEARL exits.

ANDREW looks at medal for a moment. He continues working on the clock.

EDITH comes down the stairs.

EDITH: *(Whispering.)* Good morning…

ANDREW: Good Morning.

EDITH: *(Whispering.)* Good, you're up… Don't worry about fixing the clock, George should be here any minute. You'll want to leave before Pear—

PEARL: I thought I heard voices. Good morning.

EDITH: *(Pause.)* Morning.

PEARL: Will you be joining us for breakfast?

EDITH: Breakfast?

PEARL: I know we usually fend for ourselves, but I felt like scones.

EDITH: Oh.

PEARL: *(Pause.)* While you think about that, I'll get the door.

GEORGE has just arrived at the side door. He is about to knock…

PEARL opens the door and startles GEORGE .

Good morning George.

GEORGE: Sorry!

PEARL: I'm making scones, do you want some?

GEORGE: Um…

PEARL: I'll take that as yes. Come in. Have a chair, George.

GEORGE goes to dining room table.

Sit anywhere.

He sits in "PEARL's seat".

PEARL exits to kitchen.

ANDREW stops fiddling with the clock and picks up the medal.

GEORGE: What's going on?

EDITH: I'm not sure. Charles? Do you know what's going on?

ANDREW smiles.

Well.

GEORGE: *(To ANDREW.)* I've found a place for you. It's a farm, a young couple from the States… Quakers. It will be very safe. We should— What is it?

PEARL enters.

PEARL: The scones are in the oven. Quite a storm last night.

GEORGE: Yes.

PEARL: Cleared up nicely.

GEORGE: Hmmm.

PEARL: Charles? (Do you want to ask George?)

ANDREW: *(Pause.)* George? I need your help.

GEORGE: Yes?

ANDREW: *(He shows GEORGE the medal.)* I need to return this.

EDITH: Your medal?

GEORGE: Return your Bronze Star?

ANDREW: Yeah.

GEORGE: You should— You could mail it back. That would be the safest thing to do.

ANDREW: I'm not lookin' for the safest way.

GEORGE: Right.

ANDREW: I need to… *(Pause.)* I need to do something.

GEORGE: It's not as if you can go to Washington and throw it on the steps of Capitol Hill…

ANDREW: *(Pause.)* What?

GEORGE: You should go down to Washington and throw it on the steps of Capitol Hill.

EDITH: Surely he'll get arrested?

GEORGE: He won't get arrested, not if he goes on Saturday. Not with half a million people there.

PEARL: The Peace March?

ANDREW: A soldier at a peace march?

GEORGE: Who do you think is organizing it?

ANDREW: Really?

GEORGE: They're expecting 50,000 Vietnam Vets.

EDITH: 50,000?

GEORGE: Maybe more. You're not the only one. It's not just peaceniks and hippies that are trying to stop the war.

He stops and looks to ANDREW.

ANDREW: Yeah… OK.

GEORGE: You need to think about it?

ANDREW: No. This is good… Very good.

GEORGE: Well…we should leave soon. I'll drive you there.

PEARL: All the way to Washington?

GEORGE: How else do you think he's going to get down there?

ANDREW: But, down there it's a crime to aid a deserter.

GEORGE: We'll have to make sure we don't get caught.

ANDREW: But—

GEORGE: This is a chance of a lifetime. This is history. You're not going take that away from me are you?

ANDREW: OK, George. Thank you.

GEORGE: You're welcome. *(GEORGE stands.)* We should leave within the hour.

PEARL: So soon?

GEORGE: Yeah… We'll have to take back-roads all the way. Plus, I gotta get him back into America without getting caught.

He goes to the door.

I'll be back soon. I've gotta pack up some stuff and make a call. *(To PEARL.)* Save me some scones.

GEORGE exits. The clock, still on the table, starts to chime.

EDITH: Isn't that something.

PEARL: You fixed it!

ANDREW: Not quite. Wait for it…

The clock chimes the hours, ding, ding, then a snap sound and, click, click, plonk.

Somethin's still loose.

EDITH: I forgot it chimed.

PEARL: Every hour.

EDITH: That's right…chiming away at all hours of the day…it was quite irritating.

PEARL: Yes. You should get ready to go. Get packed.

ANDREW: I didn't unpack.

PEARL: Oh.

ANDREW: It's an army thing, always ready to go.

EDITH: I'll pack some lunch for you.

EDITH exits to the kitchen.

ANDREW exits upstairs.

PEARL is left alone.

She goes to the piano.

She stares at it a long while.

ANDREW comes back down the stairs.

PEARL: *(Without looking at him.)* I'm going to sell it. *(Pause.)* It should be played.

PEARL continues to look at the piano.

ANDREW goes to the porch. He holds the screen door open for PEARL who doesn't come.

ANDREW takes out his guitar. He starts to play a Dylan song.

PEARL hears something and comes out on to the porch.

Hmmm.

ANDREW: Dylan.

PEARL: Ahhh.

ANDREW: You know Dylan?

PEARL: Wonderful poet.

ANDREW: Yes he is.

PEARL: Edith reads his Christmas story every year.

ANDREW: Dylan Thomas?

PEARL: Yes.

ANDREW: Bob Dylan.

PEARL: The other Dylan.

ANDREW: Yes, the other Dylan.

PEARL: The one that mumbles?

ANDREW: Well actu— Yeah, the one that mumbles.

PEARL: You can understand what he says?

ANDREW: Yeah.

PEARL: And you like him?

ANDREW: Yeah. A lot.

PEARL: In spite of that voice?

ANDREW: Probably because of his voice. Because the songs are about…things.

PEARL: Things…?

ANDREW: I don't know… I mean…I feel like he's speaking for me. *(Beat.)* They call him "the voice of our generation."

PEARL: And the "voice of your generation" mumbles and sings off-key?

ANDREW: Yeah, I guess he does. But you have to listen to him…listen to what he says.

PEARL: When I was young…Caruso. I made my father buy a gramophone so I could listen to Caruso records every day.

ANDREW: You had records?

PEARL: It wasn't the Dark Ages. We had records, we had electricity, we had a telephone…actually no, we didn't have a telephone. But I had records. Do you know Caruso?

ANDREW: It was all in Italian…couldn't understand it.

PEARL: You don't have to speak Italian to understand that his heart is breaking…that there is no hope… It's all about love.

ANDREW: I thought opera was all about death.

PEARL: True, they usually all die at the end! But.. but, the greatest tragedy is…love.

ANDREW: Next time I'll listen.

PEARL is lost in a moment of thought.

ANDREW sees something…

How long has it been?

PEARL: Sorry?

ANDREW: …Since you…since you played the piano?

PEARL: *(Pause.)* A lifetime.

ANDREW: Do you miss it?

PEARL: Almost every day…I miss it. *(Pause.)* I want to (play) but I… You must think me a sad old silly woman.

ANDREW: No, Ma'am, not at all.

PEARL: Pining for years over a man I knew for a few months. Who does such a thing?

ANDREW: A romantic?

PEARL: Ha. Sorry. But only a romantic would think that was romantic.

ANDREW: What was his name?

PEARL: Hmmm... His name was Randall.

ANDREW: Randall? I don't like him already.

PEARL: Actually you would like him. Everyone liked him. He was a composer. He wrote such beautiful melodies... I performed one of his compositions at Massey Hall and fell in love—with the music... not the man. He wrote a piece for me, with a note saying that it was to be played with two fingers of each hand. *(She smiles.)* When I played it, it looked like two dancers. Hmmm... She (the right hand) was very shy... He (the left hand) was strong and knew what he wanted. On the last note...they kissed.

ANDREW: That's beautiful.

PEARL: That's when I fell in love with him. He wrote the music for our wedding and I was to hear it for the first time as I walked down the aisle. I was in my wedding dress when I received a telegram. "Sorry. Can't go through with it. Heading west". Just eight words. *(Pause.)* I needed to understand. I ran to the church and found the music and played it. It was so... Beautiful. I played it over and over again. Over and over trying to understand. What did I do? It was beautiful, the tune. *(Pause.)* It hurt so much. I stopped. I just...stopped.

ANDREW: *(Pause.)* Miss Pearl?

PEARL: And now? Now it's too late.

ANDREW: It's not too late.

PEARL: It's too late… I'm too old.

ANDREW: You might still live another twenty…thirty years.

PEARL: Wouldn't that be dreadful?

There is the sound of a car arriving.

ANDREW: There's George.

PEARL: Oh…

ANDREW: Yeah.

PEARL: Do you have everything?

ANDREW: Yeah.

GEORGE enters.

GEORGE: You ready?

ANDREW: Yeah.

GEORGE: It seems you've started something.

ANDREW: What?

GEORGE: The medal. I called down to tell them that you wanted to return your medal, the guy on the phone was an ex-Marine, said he would like to join you. They're putting the word out. He said by the time we get down there, you can expect a hundred Vets to join you. We've started something.

PEARL: Good for you George.

ANDREW: I … thanks for—

GEORGE: We should head out.

ANDREW: Yeah… I just gotta say goodbye.

GEORGE: Well, Miss Gidley.

PEARL: You take care of him.

GEORGE: I will.

GEORGE grabs ANDREW's duffle bag and exits.

ANDREW: Miss Pearl I…

PEARL: You should go.

ANDREW: Yeah…

ANDREW puts his guitar in the case.

PEARL: *(Pause.)* You're very brave, you know that?

ANDREW kisses PEARL tenderly on the lips.

There is a quietly charged moment between them.

EDITH enters with scones wrapped in tin foil.

EDITH: I've packed you some scones… Do you have everything?

ANDREW: Yes, Miss Edith, I have everything.

EDITH: Thank you.

There is a toot of the horn.

ANDREW: I should…

EDITH: Yes.

ANDREW: Thank you for…everything. Goodbye Miss Edith. Goodbye Pearl.

EDITH: Goodbye Charles.

ANDREW exits to the car. We hear the sound of

doors opening and closing and the car driving away with a short toot of the horn.

EDITH waves goodbye.

Pearl?

PEARL does not seem to hear, she goes back into the house.

EDITH stays on the porch.

PEARL walks to the piano and sits on the bench. After a moment…

PEARL plays a single sustained note.

EDITH smiles.

Slow fade to black.

The End.